Confucius in the Technology Realm

Other Books by the Author

Next Practices: An Executive Guide for Education Decision Makers

Vision: The First Critical Step in Developing a Strategy for Educational Technology

Confucius in the Technology Realm

A Philosophical Approach to Your School's Ed Tech Goals

Darryl Vidal

ROWMAN & LITTLEFIELD
Lanham • Boulder • New York • London

Published by Rowman & Littlefield
A wholly owned subsidiary of The Rowman & Littlefield Publishing Group, Inc.
4501 Forbes Boulevard, Suite 200, Lanham, Maryland 20706
www.rowman.com

Unit A, Whitacre Mews, 26-34 Stannary Street, London SE11 4AB, United Kingdom

Copyright © 2015 by Darryl Vidal

All rights reserved. No part of this book may be reproduced in any form or by any electronic or mechanical means, including information storage and retrieval systems, without written permission from the publisher, except by a reviewer who may quote passages in a review.

British Library Cataloguing in Publication Information Available

Library of Congress Cataloging-in-Publication Data Is Available

ISBN 978-1-4758-2173-4 (cloth : alk. paper)
ISBN 978-1-4758-2174-1 (pbk. : alk. paper)
ISBN 978-1-4758-2175-8 (electronic)

∞™ The paper used in this publication meets the minimum requirements of American National Standard for Information Sciences—Permanence of Paper for Printed Library Materials, ANSI/NISO Z39.48-1992.

Printed in the United States of America

Contents

Foreword   vii
Michael Casey

Preface   ix

Introduction   xi

1. Concepts   1
2. The Building Blocks   5
3. Confucius in the Technology Realm   17
4. Major Concepts   31
5. Organizational Concepts   41
6. Instructional Concepts   51
7. Technical Concepts   71
8. Operational Concepts   83

Conclusion   99

About the Author   101

Foreword

Michael Casey

My friend, colleague, and coauthor Darryl Vidal uses his forty years of experience in studying Eastern philosophy and the *Tao Te Ching* to help the reader understand the paradox between Information Technology (IT) and Education Technology that has challenged the best of us in education. Is there really a dichotomy? Or, rather, a transformation that needs to occur within an organization to fully empower us as educators in the use of technologies in the classroom?

Darryl points out, "In the realm of Education Technology, we find ourselves in the ultimate battle of balance, a yin yang of education and technology. Do we speak of pedagogy and practicum or bandwidth and workloads?"

Darryl takes us through the transcendence of novice, apprentice, and master as they relate to the integration of technology in support of instruction. He is masterful in his analogy of Eastern philosophy as it relates to the roles in education of the student, teacher, and administrator.

Darryl moves us through the yin and yang to the *future state,* where the myriad of things melts into the Ultimate Embodiment of Education.

Michael Casey is the director of technology, Del Mar Union Schools, and president of Eire Group, a technology consulting solutions group.

Note: Darryl Vidal and Michael Casey coauthored *N3XT Practices: An Executive Guide for Education Decision Makers* and *Vision* (Rowman & Littlefield, 2014).

Preface

The *Tao Te Ching* is often recognized as the fundamental text of popular Eastern philosophy. As an author of the Education Technology books, *N3XT Practices* and *Vision*, Darryl Vidal has brought his professional insights to the fore. These books are pragmatic studies in Education Technology project management and strategy. They provide structure and methodology of these "less exact" sciences of Information Technology (IT) in the educational organization.

The author attempts to provide tools and processes to bring organization and discipline to educational entities where IT is often in chaos—lacking structure and strategy.

In these books, the author has drawn from over twenty-five years of experience working with schools and school districts, often as program or project manager, for highly technical and complex technology initiatives such as one-to-one computing, data center virtualization, and districtwide wireless networking.

He has also, however, drawn from over forty years of martial arts training and Eastern philosophy. The author has taught Kenpo karate, Filipino stick fighting, and is also trained in wrestling, boxing, and Wing Chun. In 2012, the author was elevated to Grandmaster Ju Dan (Tenth Degree Black Belt) under the Rosas Kenpo Karate Association.

In the martial arts world, the author is best known for his appearance in the 1980s cult classic the *Karate Kid*, where he doubles as the Mr. Miyagi character performing the "crane technique" on the wooden pilings at the beach. Vidal again appears as himself, playing the "semifinalist" character in the final tournament scenes where he can be seen winning several bouts using flashy kicking technique.

Study of the *I Ching*, the ancient book of changes, and the *Tao Te Ching* center on moving beyond the practical and physical realms, to immersion, and embodiment, and finally transcendence. How can this apply to Education Technology?

In this work, the author has decided to soften on structure and focus on art—to not only take a philosophical approach to the planning and management of the chaotic and ever-changing realm of Education Technology, but to also reinforce the ethereal concepts with real-world, familiar examples.

By melding twenty-five years of practical Education Technology consulting and program management with forty years of martial arts and Eastern philosophical teaching and training, the author offers ideas and concepts that he has used to transform schools as well as martial arts students from neophytes to outstanding examples in their field of practice.

These are concepts and methods that the author has previously kept in silos, drawing experience and methods from within their silos—but also between them—mixing concepts with processes and seeking higher benefit than merely creating a plan or progressing to the next belt level.

The ultimate objectives of impacting student learning and achievement and mastery of physiological and philosophical self-discipline becomes one and the same—thus, the Tao of Education Technology can be seen as the path to transcending the organization's people, policies, and processes to attain a state in which the whole is greater than the sum of its parts—where the Education Technology infrastructure and operational support structure are ingrained and embodied within the organization as a whole.

Its mere existence completes the organization—not an add-on structure to address technology symptoms, but an adhesive filling the gaps between departments and individuals, becoming a part of the overall organizational structure.

That is not to say that the author has infinite wisdom or can teach anyone about themselves and the meaning of life/education. Only that by using a similar mode of inquiry and verse as the ancient texts, the author offers the reader an opportunity to contemplate their day-to-day endeavors under the light of a more noble cause—the *Ultimate Embodiment*.

The Tao of Education Technology goes further to describe the Ultimate Embodiment of education within its community and, therefore, society.

Thus, where the *Tao Te Ching* and *I Ching* seek to help the individual transcend his own existence and understanding of life through love, the Tao of Education Technology seeks to allow its reader to contemplate their place within society, wherein the educational entity is an integral part of the community and society as a whole.

Sounds ethereal, doesn't it?

Introduction

The *Tao Te Ching* (pronounced Dow De Jing) is a Chinese classic text often referred to as the source for Taoism and Chinese philosophy. According to tradition, the sage Lao Tzu, meaning "Old Master," a record keeper at the Zhou dynasty court, wrote it around the sixth century BC. The text's true authorship and date of composition or compilation are still debated, although the oldest excavated text dates back to the late fourth century BC.

The text is fundamental for both philosophical and religious Taoism, and it strongly influenced other schools, such as Confucianism and Chinese Buddhism. Many Chinese artists including poets, painters, calligraphers, and even gardeners have used the *Tao Te Ching* as a source of inspiration. Its influence has also spread widely outside East Asia, and it is among the most translated works in world literature.

Confucius was a teacher, editor, and philosopher living in the 551 to 479 BC era of Chinese history.

The philosophy of Confucius emphasized personal and societal morality, correctness of societal relationships, and justice. Confucius is traditionally credited with having authored or edited many of the Chinese classic texts; however, modern scholars rarely attribute specific verses or quotes to Confucius himself. Most often refer to his teachings as ancient Chinese wisdom communicated through "fortune cookies."

Confucius's principles had a basis in common Asian traditions and beliefs. He advocated loyalty to family, worship of ancestors, and respect of elders by their children and of husbands by their wives.

Confucius is best known for espousing the well-known principle "Do not do to others what you do not want done to yourself," an early reversed version of the Golden Rule.

What do these ancient philosophers have to do with Education Technology?

Well, nothing—and everything.

As we look at the ever-changing dynamic, of technology and its applications in education, it becomes difficult to "see the forest for the trees." This means that it is easy to lose sight of the vision and strategy and to focus too much on the nuts, bolts, speeds, and feeds of the technology surrounding day-to-day interactions, both in occupational and social settings.

But education, as an entity within its community, is currently evolving and sustaining in a whirlwind of technology upheaval. Never has the demand from community to embrace "things/devices/technology" been as strong as in today's twenty-first-century school.

This is not just true for IT directors. It applies to all connected to the education process—teachers, administrators, staff, and ultimately the students—who are the presumptive benefactors of all this great "stuff."

Can you ever remember your school or district talking about buying adding machines or typewriters or calculators for every single student? Yet today, every single school is planning some sort of infrastructure and device strategy for their students. And parents are asking why their children have no access to devices when at home or wireless networking when in the gym.

For Education Technologists, this becomes the critical success factor. You may have launched the most successful deployment of one-to-one devices in your state, with a minimum of quad-core Intel processor, 4GB of static RAM, 500GB of hard drive storage, and 802.11n wireless to stream live video through your tablet to the projector for each student, *but*, how did it impact student achievement? Did test scores rise?

In the review of these ancient philosophies, Taoism and Confucianism, we don't find answers. How could a civilization 2,500 years before us have any concept of how to deal with today's Education Technology challenges? There was no student information system, no wireless security, no gradebook, or disk archival systems necessary in 500 BC.

What we do find are methods of inquiry—mental exercises that can be performed to examine our daily endeavors, as well as lifelong pursuits, under the light of the ultimate goal. In life that goal may be spiritual, philosophical, or practical, or ultimately a combination or balanced mixing of these.

But in the Education Technology realm these whimsical, ethereal concepts may be the key to tactical, strategic, and visionary success, what the Tao of Ed Tech understands to be the Ultimate Embodiment—education and technology as key elements in a whole of society.

Chapter 1

Concepts

YIN AND YANG

Yin and yang can be thought of as complementary forces—but is commonly thought of as *opposing* forces—that interact to form a dynamic system wherein the whole is greater than the sum of its parts.

According to Taoist concept and the *I Ching*, everything in life and nature has both yin and yang aspects: good versus bad, light versus dark, hard versus soft, cold versus hot, and more.

Either of the two major aspects may manifest more strongly in a particular object, depending on the criterion of the observation. The yin yang shows a balance between two opposites with a little bit in each.

The *I Ching* also defines elements of earth that are represented by trigrams and are most commonly recognized: Heaven and Earth, Fire and Water, Lake and Mountain, and Thunder and Wind.

Figure 1.1 I Ching—Yin Yang. *Source*: Google images—licensed for use

The balance of all things becomes a thing of beauty, the ultimate dynamic of life and love in the universe.

We deal with the yin yang in almost every task and activity in our daily lives. Should I:

- get up early and feel tired? Or sleep in a little and feel energized, but be late for work?
- drive faster to try to get to work on time and risk getting a ticket? Or just drive slowly and get to work safely, but late?
- go back to school and get my degree?

The Education Technologist also has his very unique experience like these yin yang conundrums. Should I:

- take this call from the superintendent's secretary? Or ask her to call the help desk?
- use a private or public cloud?
- implement wireless saturation in one school? Or just wireless coverage in all schools?
- invest in infrastructure or devices?
- use Office 365? Or GAFE?

Each option has its positives and negatives. The balance must be found between appeasing the masses and managing the enterprise.

Each teacher, administrator, or staff has their own yin yang to balance each and every day. So we can see why it is very easy to lose sight of the forest when you're flying through the trees at Mach 2 and hitting one tree could blow up the whole ship.

So, let's take a deep breath and step away from the steering wheel, and let a moment of clarity encompass our thoughts.

In the study and practice of Education Technology, the yin yang concepts are also the key to success or failure, promotion or unemployment.

As you read the Tao of Education Technology, we will see that the yin yang once again displays itself in the ultimate balance of organization and society, structure versus flexibility, authority versus autonomy, tools versus thought.

Let us also take a moment to revel in the beauty of this balance. Without this balance, what would it mean for community and society as a whole?

Everything we perceive and interact with presents us with a yin yang conflict, or rather, balance.

Let's look a scenario that is near and dear to our collective Ed Tech hearts.

MISSIONS, GOALS, OBJECTIVES, PHILOSOPHIES, AND TRANSCENDENCE

Any strategy or planning process always begins with a definition of goals and objectives. More loftier plans may start by defining a mission statement.

Consultants make their living leading their clients through brainstorming sessions and self-examination exercises to develop the ethereal concepts that embody the ultimate success as defined for *their* endeavor, their vision.

These necessary processes and their resultant precepts, well communicated, ensure that all stakeholders recognize the same common goals—that they are marching to the same drum, and that their ultimate success is understood, shared, and clearly serves the greater good of not just the organization but of the community wherein it exists.

Taoism follows a similar yet reverse-order approach—the yin yang approach, if you will. One of the reasons for this bottom-up phenomenon is the acknowledgment by the novice that they do not know, or understand, what the higher-order objective really is, that without experiencing dark, then light, they would never understand life and love—also known as transcendence—the movement from a noun state (being or existing as one self within a society) to a verb state (progressive but transitionary) to the ultimate or future being/existence (or nonexistence), being one with the universe, part of and not.

This becomes a quandary, most often for IT staff who may be directed to work toward the "greater good"—a commonly accepted term for doing the right thing for the students—but without a clear vision of what this "greater good" really is, how can the staff member really use this concept to guide their actions?

In today's education universe, schools and educators are under immense pressure to jump on the bandwagon of technology initiatives, however ill-advised they may be. The current headlines regarding some very large school districts obligate the need to address and readdress the wisdom behind many of these large-scale technology purchases, specifically one-to-one programs in which long-term bond debt is used for devices that have a three-year life.

The Education Technology strategy must be rooted in the educational mission, goals, and objectives. Thus the educational mission should define the *ultimate goal*—a total embodiment of education within the community it serves—society. Thus, this ultimate goal of education and its inherent role within society is referred to by the Tao of Ed Tech as the *Ultimate Embodiment*—the educational dynamic as a key element within society as a whole.

Where the novice finds himself as one within the classroom, the apprentice as one within a school of novices and apprentices, where the master is one among masters, and the enablers are bound to their scopes, where their goal is to achieve the near-term success, the goal of the headmaster and community (society) is to meld them all into a single, universal dynamic.

It is where each player clearly understands his or her role within the near-scope while learning and becoming responsible and productive members of society.

In the following chapter—The Building Blocks—we will examine concepts and ideas expressed in the Tao of Ed Tech, the epochs or stages of the yin yang concepts, and map them accordingly to Ed Tech concepts. Of course, one could question the logic of the philosophical concepts mapping to a practical need and organizational dynamic.

But what we find in the fog of chaos is that it is often the transcendence beyond tasks and responsibilities that allows the organization to become more than the sum of its parts, to go beyond the simple near-scopes of each team member's interest and expertise.

In the doom of complexity, it is not the minutiae that will guide and deliver us, but the clarity of thought and direction. And although the devil is in the details, what defines the details but vision and strategy?

Chapter 2

The Building Blocks

This chapter will examine concepts, rules, and ideas, both from the philosophical as well as the practical, from Eastern thought and from Education Technology. And as we delve further into these concepts, we will constantly be struck by the relevance and criticality of thought, direction, and constancy.

THE MYRIAD OF THINGS

The Tao of Education Technology refers often to the *myriad of things*, just as the *Tao Te Ching* often refers to the *ten thousand things* or *myriad things*. So what are these things?

In the *I Ching* realm, the *ten thousand things* call on the material things surrounding man: water, soil, stone, wood, implements, shelter, and more.

These myriad things comprise the world in which we live in. They are things to be acted upon, to be used, turned into tools, implements, weapons, turned into shelter, home buildings, and banks.

Once again, the myriad things become a focus for the uninitiated, but blur into our surroundings as we take the ethereal view. And upon transcendence, they become everything, and nothing.

Which of these *myriad things* are required for knowing one's self and one's position in the world?

To the Education Technologist, the myriad of things becomes all the technological things that may pervade the classroom and school. Everything from pencil and paper to projector, document camera, to laptops and apps, and of course, devices, devices, devices—computers, tablets, smartphones, and more.

It can also be immediately recognized that students, teachers, administrators, Ed Tech and IT staff can all easily lose strategic focus by becoming immersed in the myriad of things.

Students worrying about having the latest app, teachers with the latest tools (toys), Ed Techies with their latest software gadgets, and IT with their latest web filter configuration—all are focused on the myriad of things, and are part of the Ultimate Embodiment, inasmuch as the "thing" becomes a means to an "achievement" end result.

When all are too focused on their "things," the Ultimate Embodiment contracts to less than the sum of the various and individual parts—moving in not any specific direction—where dysfunction pervades and chaos reigns. But when all regard their "things" as a means to the greater goal, then the whole of the participants becomes necessarily greater than the sum of its parts, and the Ultimate Embodiment becomes.

BLOOM'S TAXONOMY

Bloom's taxonomy defines "domains" of learning (cognitive, affective, and psychomotor), each of which is organized as a hierarchy.

It suggests that mastery must be achieved at the lower levels in order to progress to and address the higher levels (a bottom-up approach of skills development). In addition to providing a sequential model for approaching the curriculum, it also suggests a method to categorize levels of learning, in terms of the expected understanding for a given subject matter. Thus, in the cognitive domain, training for technicians may cover technical knowledge, comprehension, and application but not concern itself with analysis and creativity, whereas full professional training may be expected to include all the higher-level skills defined in the model.

The Cognitive Domain of Bloom's taxonomy represents a continuum of increasing cognitive complexity—from remembering to analyzing, evaluating, and creating.

In further chapters, we will examine the epochs as a continuum of states. We can identify the lower levels of Bloom's taxonomy as the rudimentary or yin state, the middle levels as the yang state, and the highest levels as the future or new state, the ultimate level of cognitive practicum. These will make more sense later.

As educators, Bloom's taxonomy is a fundamental model not only for the student but also the teacher. It is not necessary for the student to be aware of the cognitive model, only that the teacher strives to instruct in a way that allows the student to achieve the higher-level skills of analyzing, evaluating, and creating. Therefore, the cognitive skills are not the objective,

The Building Blocks

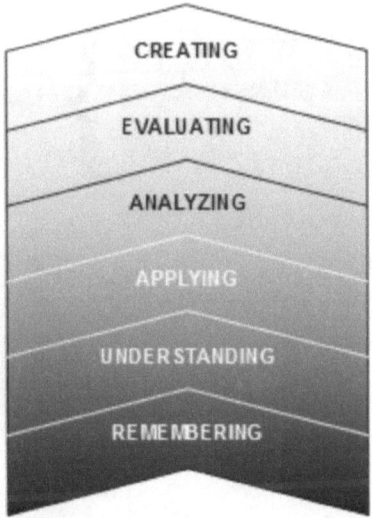

Figure 2.1 Cognitive Domain of Bloom's Taxonomy. *Source*: Visio drawing–dvidal

but the resultant development of analysis and critical thinking modeled by the practicum using the curriculum.

This is reinforced not only by curriculum but by practice, and the only way for an entire school site or district to embody these higher-level skills is by first identifying them as goals and objectives, then defining them (or something like them) in a communicable format, modeling them in a way that the curriculum and practice is in a standard and deliverable format, and providing a program that is constantly improving and reinforcing—a precept of the Tao of Ed Tech.

This is a professional development curriculum focused on developing student's higher-level cognitive skills, structured in successive PD courses and templates, and reinforced throughout the school year.

The final critical success factor is improved student achievement and—dare we say it?—higher test scores.

SAMR—TECHNOLOGICAL IMPACT

The Substitution Augmentation Modification Redefinition model defines the potential impact of computer technology on teaching and learning. The model proposes that at the lowest levels of technology integration (into the curriculum, not into the classroom), the technological impact is nothing more than enhancement of communication.

An example is when a teacher uses a document camera in the exact same way they used to use an overhead projector.

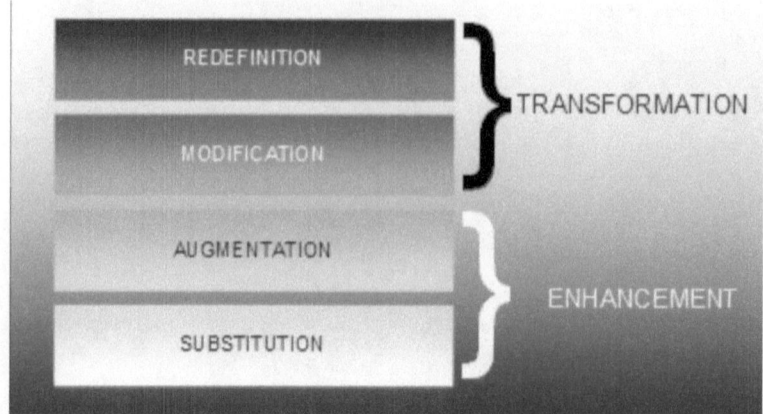

Figure 2.2 Ruben R. Puentedura, PhD, defines these levels of technology integration.
Source: Visio drawing–dvidal

As the teacher learns to become more effective using the technology, the curriculum undergoes a transformation where the pedagogy and work engender a transformational impact—for example, using collaboration software to transform a lecture group from discussion to online and remote interaction.

It is important to note that each teacher individually will deal with the challenge of learning to use available technology tools to engender moving the students up the cognitive model. Access and availability of tools is mandatory to enable transformation.

It becomes the responsibility of Education Technology to model the professional development that allows the teachers to leapfrog this testing and inquiry process that immediately allows both the teacher and the students to work at the top of the SAMR model.

THE EPOCHS

The *Tao Te Ching* also describes the balance of opposing forces as a progression of mankind from savage to citizen and then to enlightenment—transcendence. We spoke of it lightly in the Bloom's taxonomy discussion, now it will make more sense.

This is related through the yin, yang, and new (future) epochs—transformational phases of societal complexity.

The Yin Epoch

The yin epoch may be defined as the time period from the beginning of man through to early social constructs.

This is when mankind's existence started, as a base-level existence. Hunting, gathering, living in small familial groups—the yin epoch. Also known as the "noun" state, it is man's simplest form or existence, yet arguably it is as close to transcendence as any other state.

This is where man's lack of cognitive experience and reality actually stands him closer to nature and his universe.

But man is unable to achieve enlightenment, or transcendence, without passing through the yang phase.

The Yang Epoch

The yang epoch may be seen as the time period from the first governments and societies through today.

As mankind developed from hunting and gathering to the organization of villages and communities, the rules and laws and philosophies had also become more complex and progressive—the yang epoch, also referred to as the "verb" state.

This is the progression from simplicity to complexity. Where governments are formed to allow men to lead and force others to follow. This is the epoch farthest from transcendence because of man's focus on the myriad of things—the complexities of life.

Think of your own life, of your day-to-day activities and awareness. Driving, attending, participating, leading, following—these are all activities that encompass our current existence.

We do, however, teach and remind ourselves of the concepts and roles of the greater existence, the universal truth of nature, when we say things like:

- "Take the time to smell the roses."
- "Be one with nature."
- "Find beauty in all of nature."
- "Become one with nature."

Although we may take these opportunities to be one with nature and appreciate the finer things in life, we are always quickly brought back into our yang epoch, whenever we need to pay the bills, shop for groceries, or slam on the brakes.

We may be stuck in the yang epoch, but that does not prevent us from seeking the universal truth—just because we need to live in the real world doesn't mean we can't seek enlightenment or a universal truth.

The New Epoch

The new epoch may become reality in some future time. One day in the future, all men will transcend earth and material things and know life

	Yin	Yang	New
Bloom's Taxonomy	Memory	Creating	Encompassing
SAMR	Enhancement	Transformation	Remodeled
Teacher Technology	Tools	Multimedia	Multi-Modal
Student Devices	Laptop/Tablet	Device Flexible	Device Independence
Information Technology	Staff	Reactive	Proactive
Educational Technology	Productivity Skills	Enhancement	Ingrained
Mentoring/Coaching	Outlines / Syllabus	Leading Leaders	Acting as One
Planning	Planning	Understanding	All Being

Figure 2.3 Ed Tech conceptual progression visio–dvidal.

through love—the new epoch (also referred to as the future epoch or "future state").

In the Tao of Ed Tech, we understand this new epoch, or future state, as the Ultimate Embodiment. Not only does each participant understand his or her role in the educational realm, but also in society as a whole. It is where educational indoctrination is efficient and effective. Where students achieve and successfully transition from indoctrination to productive citizens who then take on their own roles within society.

The following table examines Education Technology concepts and components of the environment and offers a progression from noun state, to verb state, to future state.

ROLES, PARTICIPANTS

The Tao of Education Technology defines roles in parallel with our current educational participants: students, teachers, support staff, and administrators. These roles are referred to in the Tao of Education Technology as novice, apprentice, enablers, and master, respectively.

All have a critical role within the organization. It becomes of the utmost importance that each understands his or her role and its criticality.

Without this context, the myriad of things begins to take over and become the focus. With this context, the myriad of things melts into the Ultimate Embodiment of education within the community via its participants.

How can we benefit community, or the whole of society, without raising the participants to a higher level? And it becomes more obvious in this context that all participants are just as key as the object participant—the novice. Each has a role to play, a benefit to offer, as well as to extract or exploit.

Novice

The novice is the subject of our endeavors. It is he who follows the path, who seeks the objective, but he is not alone—he shares the same objectives as his many peers.

The novice, however, is not ignorant of the Ultimate Embodiment; he is already part of it, without knowing. He becomes the key player in the Ultimate Embodiment.

The novice can be seen as passing from the yin phase of "being"—being totally ignorant of speech, grammar, arts, sciences—to the yang phase of "progressing" or learning—to the new phase, or Ultimate Embodiment—where the novice becomes apprentice, and then master.

He may be a master within the educational context or outside. But you can see how the cycle continues.

Apprentice

The moniker of apprentice is not meant to diminish the teacher. In fact, the designation is meant to communicate the intimate relationship between novice and apprentice—student and teacher.

The interaction between novice and apprentice is at once intimate and interactive. The apprentice communicates curriculum to the novice using pedagogy—pedagogy learned and communicated.

The interaction between student and teacher becomes the model of multiple interactions, enabled in time and complexity by technology. Think of the process of homework submission, review, revision, and continued revision based on this interaction.

Technology has a marked impact on this relationship, both directly and indirectly.

Examples of the revolutionizing impact of technology on the relationship of the student and teacher is best offered by the use of collaborative word processing tools, in which a student can submit a homework project electronically and the teacher can review it and offer suggestions in real-time immediacy. This level of real-time interactive teaching is what we describe in *N3XT Practices*, the true manifestation of one-to-one computing. But it is not in the context of one student to one device; it's in the context of one teacher to one student, which is codified and enabled by using collaborative and mobile device tools.

Master

The principal or site administrator equates to the master in the Tao of Education Technology. He leads the apprentices in their endeavors with their novices. He communicates the Ultimate Embodiment context to the apprentices, who in turn embody these concepts in leading their novices. In essence, the leadership context of the master is passed to the apprentice, and then to the novice.

The master also interacts with the novices, but in a more indirect and figurehead role—critical that it is.

The master must lead the apprentices through one of the four techniques discussed in the leadership chapter. And he passes these traits, whether positive or negative, on to his organization from the top-down.

These four leadership contexts described by the Tao of Ed Tech are also similar to those in the chapters of the *Tao Te Ching*.

Other similarities may be found between the two texts, but it is not a plagiaristic instance, only that the core of the descriptions are similar in both realms, much as we would all individually describe the sky as blue.

Enabler

In the *Tao Te Ching*, the concept of enabler is not explored, as many externalities are considered part of the *ten thousand things*, but in the context of the educational organization/district, we can understand the wide cast of supporting staff.

The enablers are any of a number of supporting administrative, instructional, and operational personnel including IT staff, Ed Technology staff, custodians, bus drivers, and others. Although not discrete players in the apprentice/novice relationship, the endeavors of the novices and apprentices cannot be realized without the support and sustainment of the enablers.

Just as the apprentices, the enablers are more directly influenced by the master and/or headmaster. They follow the restrictive or liberal policies of their leadership and mentors. By "enabling" the enablers, the master supports the needs and objectives of the apprentices and novices. Without this support, the apprentices are forced to teach and communicate with their novices without the use of leveraged and advanced tools and techniques.

And just as the novices and apprentices, their roles are critical to the success of the organization. Just remember the time the network went down, and the IT enablers had to not only bring it back up but also harden and maintain it.

Headmaster

The headmaster represents the district superintendent of schools, the ultimate leader within the educational enterprise. But the headmaster does not represent the top of the hierarchy since the educational enterprise is merely a spoke in the wheel of the greater community.

THE PARADOXES

Man and nature experience many paradoxes, instances in which one aspect seems to negate or reverse another, such as good and evil, knowledge and wisdom, clarity and incoherence. We experience all these aspects in nature and our life directly.

"How am I supposed to learn all these subjects while continuing to focus on the greater good?"

"How can I understand the theory of gravity, while pondering the meaning of life?"

"How can I learn to use this laptop while not exposing my students to my technological ignorance?"

"How can I manage this complex network, and still provide the teachers the flexibility to choose their own software platforms?"

"How can I achieve Common Core standards while still teaching my students about ethics and good citizenship?"

Figure 2.4 Drawing by Bradley Vidal. *Source*: Bradley Vidal

All of these examples are daily struggles we may face, but in all cases, the latter negates the former only if we let it.

Their yin and yang existence is one that can be easily transcended merely by living in the real world while acknowledging the ultimate importance of truth and society.

THE PARADOX OF LANGUAGE

Just as the *Tao Te Ching* immediately encounters a paradox, or conflict of ideas, the Tao of Education Technology encounters similar and dissimilar paradoxes. The first and most obvious in both realms is language.

From the first chapter of the *Tao Te Ching*:

> The Tao that can be told is not the eternal Tao
> The name that can be named is not the eternal Name.
> The unnamable is the eternally real.
> Naming is the origin of all particular things.

You can already hear the Tao struggle with the limitation of words. Words have meanings defined by men. But what if men don't understand the true meaning of the world in which they live? More directly, what if men don't understand the world in which they live? Which takes us to this conclusion: men can't understand the world in which they live.

Yet they try to define it using a language developed by men that don't understand their world. Can their language ever hope to embody the universe?

The first critical step in strategy development is always this definition of goals. To define the goal, we use words. Here we arrive at the first paradox of Education Technology.

In the realm of Ed Tech, we find ourselves in the ultimate battle of balance, a yin yang of education and technology. Do we speak of pedagogy and practicum or bandwidth and workloads?

The Education Technology paradox is ingrained in the educational organization and its inherent challenge is to define the appropriate chain of command. Who leads the techies?

THE PARADOX OF IT AND ED TECH

So we see that the dilemma of technology in the learning environment is a conundrum from its core. Its inherent cost and cost of ownership is a capital expenditure like no other the school has faced, going back to Persia.

The Building Blocks

Let's take a stab at it:

- Information Technology is the organization responsible for managing infrastructure, information services, maintenance, and support of computing and technology equipment.
- Education Technology is the organization responsible for supporting technology pedagogy and instructional technology professional development.

If we examine each school district's definition of IT and Ed Tech, these distinctions become glaring.

In these organizational charts, we see varying degrees of centralized leadership for IT and Ed Tech.

In the legacy organization, Figure 2.5a, which to a large degree still defines many or most smaller-sized school districts, we see the IT techies working under business and the Ed Techies working under curriculum. Although there is no reason this cannot be successful, we can see that there is an organizational divide that must be overcome in order to align the priorities of these two disparate departments.

In the modern organization, Figure 2.5b, we see technology elevated to the cabinet level, garnering its own resources and mindshare at the leadership level. This org chart may be recognized in some medium-to-large school districts in an attempt to prioritize technology within the school/district. But is this flawed organizational thinking?

In the modern, evolved organization, Figure 2.5c, we see Ed Tech and IT consolidated under curriculum. This organization does two things:

1. It aligns the objectives and priorities of Ed Tech and IT under a single curriculum leader.
2. It demotes technology as a department from the cabinet level.

I have been quoted, more than once, saying: "If I were the IT director, I would want to be the CIO (Figure 2.5b), but if I were the superintendent, I would not want the techie in the cabinet (Figure 2.5c)."

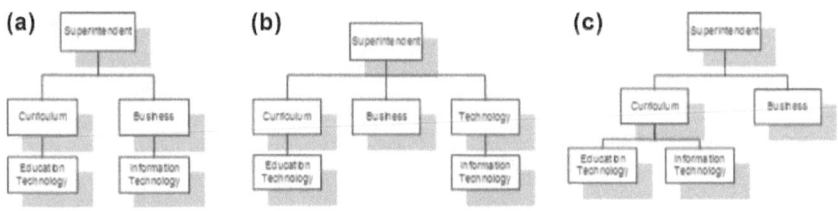

Figure 2.5 **Figure #s embedded in graphic.** *Source*: Visio drawing – dvidal

This thinking acknowledges the concept that technology, in and of itself, is not a center-point objective or a cabinet-level department. Technology is simply a set of tools used to make instruction more effective, and it can be well represented as a priority in the cabinet by the curriculum, facilities, or business leader.

That's not to say that any of these examples is more successful than the other, only that leadership becomes the critical success factor in any of these organizational scenarios.

So the good news is, you don't have to change your organization, just the dynamic of leadership, objectives, and priorities.

FINAL NOTES

As we prepare to delve into the passages of the Tao of Ed Tech, we must address the relevance, or irrelevance, of the historical and religious aspects of Taoism and Confucianism. Taoism and Confucianism have existed together in China for well over two thousand years. Both Confucianism and Taoism are rooted in the *I Ching*, the ancient book of Changes. Both had their roots in philosophy and developed religious aspects as they evolved.

Both are considered philosophies and religions of China. Their founders, Confucius and Lao Tzu (Taoism), were contemporaries of ancient China—circa 600 to 500 BCE (Before the Common Era).

Confucianism centers on social matters, while Taoism focuses on the search for meaning. They share common ideas about man, society, and transcendence, although these notions were around long before either philosophy.

Legend holds that Confucius and Lao Tzu did meet to discuss the Imperial Archives. Lao Tzu was not impressed by Confucius's elaborate robes and preferred a more monastic existence in order to achieve transcendence.

Thus the following text—The Tao of Education Technology—may be thought of as the product of the ancient method of inquiry that both Confucius and Lao Tzu may have used to build their analects and key concepts.

Chapter 3

Confucius in the Technology Realm
The Tao Education Technology

Figure 3.1 *Source*: Google images—licensed for use

ON EDUCATION

What is education but a plan for the future?
A plan wherein everyone has a role, be it novice, apprentice, enabler,
    or master.
A plan wherein facts become subjects, and subjects become disciplines.
A plan that accounts for all, that engages all, that encompasses all.
A plan to know the Ultimate Embodiment.
Where disciplines are defined and assessed.
Where assessment leads to evaluation and determination.
Where success becomes personal achievement.
Where achievement becomes a new plan that begins the process over again.
Where novice becomes apprentice then master of his own domain
    in society.
Where the Ultimate Embodiment is known, then forgotten.

The whole of the education universe, however global or nationalized, is really a community-based phenomenon. Local Control and Accountability Plans (LCAPs) are required in California for school districts to engage with their students, parents, and communities and to develop a plan that addresses eight priorities:

1. Providing all students access to fully credentialed teachers, instructional materials that align with state standards, and safe facilities.
2. Implementation of academic standards, including the Common Core State Standards in English language arts and math, next generation science standards, English language development, history and social science, visual and performing arts, and health education and physical education standards.
3. Encourage parent involvement and participation so the local community is engaged in the decision-making process and the educational programs of students.
4. Improving student achievement and outcomes along multiple measures, including test scores, English proficiency, and college and career preparedness.
5. Supporting student engagement, including whether students attend school or are chronically absent.
6. Highlighting school climate and connectedness through a variety of factors, such as suspension and expulsion rates and other locally identified means.
7. Ensuring all students have access to classes that prepare them for college and careers, regardless of what school they attend or where they live.
8. Measuring other important student outcomes related to required areas of study, including physical education and the arts.

Beyond these types of local accountability programs comes the underlying perceived requirements of education in the community:

- Equity
- Standards compliance
- Parental and community involvement
- Focus on student achievement
- Student engagement
- School climate and connectedness
- Career/college preparation
- Other outcomes

The LCAP standard requirements are a great starting point for Education Technology strategy, but are they enough? Of course not. That is the point of parental community involvement.

These and other national and statewide standards are what we refer to as external inputs to the technology strategic planning process.

The Tao understands that education as an idea is nothing but a lesson plan with a goal. But it is also a critical component to the community/society as a whole to provide for guided indoctrination to become a productive part of society.

It is where the educational entity is not a parallel agency existing for itself, but an integral part of community, woven through every aspect, part of, within.

Therefore, the Ultimate Embodiment of education within society is transcendence defined by the Tao of Education Technology.

ON TECHNOLOGY

What is technology but a tool? An implement no more important than the novice's pencil and paper, or the chalk and board upon which the apprentice demonstrates.
What of the pencil and paper? The chalk and board?
What is the significance of one without the other?
What is the effect of one with the other?
Once the novice utilizes the pencil upon the paper, has any problem been solved? Wrong righted? Need fulfilled?
Once the apprentice's chalk acts upon the board, what of the apprentice?
Has the novice learned? Achieved?
The tools cannot enable the apprentice to assess and evaluate just as the application of pencil upon the paper doesn't enable the student to propose and solve. It is at once a memorial and a message. A question answered but the result undetermined.
It is but part of the myriad of things.
These implements are meaningless without context.
The context is given but is it received?
But there is more to the pencil than its application upon the paper, or the chalk upon the board.
The expression of thoughts penciled on the paper by the novice can be quintessentially wrong or right. The demonstration of chalk upon board can be valid or not.
The application of the myriad of things for teaching and learning can be equally beneficial or flawed.

We've had it drilled into our heads since the early days of computing in education—*It's not about the technology*. But in this passage, we understand the yin and yang for technology tools.

Although they aren't the focus, they must first be, for I cannot write without sharpening the pencil, just as I cannot write on the laptop without first knowing how to turn it on and double-click on the word processor.

Yet to hear endless discussions and debate surrounding one-to-one computing and BYOD (bring your own device), one would think that every school and teacher is concerned about what type of device will be used in the classroom. This is like asking what is the best pen to write with.

What series of inquiry could be more flawed? This technological debate is like going to the fishing tackle store without knowing where you are going fishing and what you are fishing for.

How could one technology tool be the right one for every student, in every school, and every curriculum? Answer: It can't and won't.

But in the example of the pencil and paper, we see a different, more noble entreaty. The use of tools so fundamental as to be simple enough to be used by every student to solve any problem and detail any solution.

In essence, the pencil and paper has achieved something that the tablet and laptop for the classroom has not: the ability to be all things to all people.

And this is strictly because of the complexity of the technology tool in and of itself.

Although we tend to tune these issues out, the issues surrounding student technology and computing are anything but simple and all encompassing.

Consider the questions regarding classroom laptops for students. Here is a list of IT considerations for deployment and support (compare these considerations to the pencil and paper example):

- device and operating system
- networking and connectivity—infrastructure
- applications and compatibility
- user support
- device support
- repair and preventive maintenance
- warrantees
- salvage and replacement

This myriad of considerations doesn't even take into account the curriculum and the classroom management questions. "What of the pencil and paper?"

What would it take to render classroom technology to be as simple and useable as pencil and paper?

ON EDUCATION TECHNOLOGY

What of education technology?
We do not speak of education AND technology as if these two words when used sequentially connote a higher form.
Is education changed by technology? If so, is this good?
Is technology a type of education? If so, what of schools?
In the Ultimate Embodiment of education, what of technology?
The pencil and paper?

In our book, *N3XT Practices*, we bluntly stated,

> These words go together like biscuits and gravy, yet schools are plagued by insufficient study into one area by the other. This comparison works both ways—most educators don't have a deep understanding of technology or how it all works together, while technologists don't understand education from the educator's perspective. This conceptual divide typically results in the following outcomes:
>
> 1. Money spent on technology without specific curricular planning—meaning little or no resultant benefit to student learning or academic results, or a result that can't be measured by a means that is reliable and defensible.
> 2. Technology that cannot be used effectively because of lack of infrastructure, and finally
> 3. Technology in the classroom that the teacher hasn't been trained to use effectively.
>
> —*N3XT Practices: An Executive Guide for Education Decision Makers*
> (Rowman & Littlefield Education, 2014)

We cannot let Education Technology be a focus in and of itself, much like STEM (science, technology, math, and engineering) is not the "study of," but rather ingrained within the curriculum.

Education Technology *must* connote leveraging advanced tools to facilitate student learning and achievement to where the resultant outcome includes one or more of the following complements:

- advanced analytical and critical-thinking skills leveraged by the use of technology
- collaboration and group work facilitated by technology
- improved outcomes and test scores aided by technology tools' availability
- enhanced equity and access using technology tools
- and more.

ON VISION

What is the vision for the future? Was there a vision for the past?
Where was this vision? Who made the vision? Can a vision be created?
   Is it made by someone?
Is the vision technology tools in every classroom, for every student? To what end?
Is the vision for an ultimate ethereal existence—at one with the universe?
Is the vision for achievement, of the novice? Of family, community, and society?
It is all, and it is none.

A vision is one of the most important aspects of any endeavor, entity, or organization, yet that is not to say that one of these cannot exist without a vision or be successful without a vision.

A vision is a plan, general and encompassing enough for everyone to take part and to understand their critical roles, but also specific enough to detail a specific path, a strategy for attainment, a functional and realistic road map.

But what of this plan? If your organization is wise enough to develop this vision, what to do with it? What role does the vision fulfill? How does it help any individual?

Success without a vision is just luck!

ON VISION DEVELOPMENT

Where from comes the vision? What form comes the vision? Do not assume this vision, for although it may be fundamental, it is not detailed and specific for the novice, the apprentice, the enabler.
Whom must create the vision? Whom does the vision serve?
What spurns the development of the vision? And its role in the Ultimate Embodiment.
The leader of leaders, leads without leading—driven toward a vision, that all must understand, know and embody.

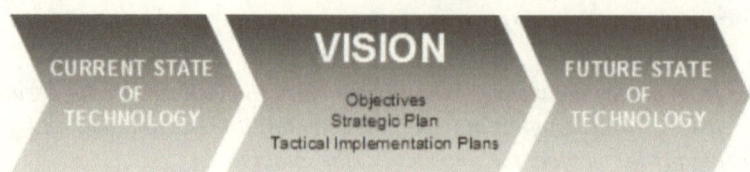

Figure 3.2   *Source*: Visio drawing – dvidal

In our last book, *Vision*, the first critical step in developing a strategy for Educational Technology, we wrote extensively on the process of developing a vision for technology application within your school. The vision cannot be assumed.

It is common sense to work toward a "common good." But this alone does not provide a vision. Of course, the key element of developing an Education Technology vision is "education," not "technology." The vision needs to not only reflect the educational focus but also embody the essence of the objectives your school is endeavoring to achieve with instructional practices.

We hear a lot about Twenty-First-Century Learning and Common Core Standards. How do they fit into your vision? How will you embody the pillars of Common Core and Twenty-First-Century Learning practices?

Somehow the vision needs to weave in the concepts' collaboration, communication, critical thinking, and creativity. If these Common Core precepts are not included in the vision, then how are you supporting instructional practices in your district with the integration of technology?

A lot of school districts have rushed to get technology into students' hands without really having a vision for how these devices support the districts' instructional practices. Without a clear vision that supports instruction, chaos reigns.

The Education Technology vision is a product of the need to move from a current state to a defined future state. The process of defining the current state requires the discovery process and inquiry. The process of defining the future state requires a similar inquiry process but based on curricular goals and objectives. And finally, the gap analysis will define the strategy and tactics required to move from the current state to the future defined state.

What does that all mean? It's the butterfly effect in practice—the finer details ultimately define the scope of the vision and, in turn, the vision helps all participants and stakeholders understand the objectives, strategy, tactics, tasks, and activities.

ON VISION COMMUNICATION

Once these questions are answered, then, what is done with the vision? What good is a map that is kept safe in the drawer? What of the speech written but never delivered?

The vision must be hailed from the mountaintop by the headmaster. It must be repeated around the campfire by the apprentices. It must be part of the novice's indoctrination. Each enabler must understand their role in support of the vision.

The vision is where all become leaders without leading. Where all are novices and all are masters. Where all are the Ultimate Embodiment.

The vision is the Ultimate Embodiment and the Ultimate Embodiment is the vision.

So you say you've got a vision. That must mean that there is a document, diagram, and verbiage, as well as understanding, that embodies this "vision."

That must mean that the process of developing this "vision" was intentional, methodical, sponsored, and now must be endorsed by leadership.

This endorsement must come in the form of a communications plan.

From a project management standpoint, any communications plan must define the following communications:

- formal written communications—a newsletter or monthly report
- informal written communications—electronic mail distribution lists and department communications
- formal verbal communications—all hands and state of the district/school meetings
- informal verbal communications—department meetings, team meetings, work group meetings

The communications plan must define:

- who is to communicate to whom
- the method of communication
- the frequency of communication
- the designation of action items and responsibility

If all parties understand their various responsibilities regarding communications, then they can be part of the delivery and overall effectiveness. If communication is undefined and unclear, then chaos will reign.

If all parties align their communications with the vision, then there will be less dissention and open objection. And when dissention and objection exist, the communications plan must define the type and method of discussion and alignment.

Nothing can be more powerful than a vision understood and shared by all. This is where the whole truly becomes more than the sum of its parts, where individuals transcend their individuality and become one with their role within the community.

Chapter 4

Major Concepts

ON THE MYRIAD OF THINGS

What do we see? What do we touch? What do we use?
What of the myriad of things?
Do these things define us? Do they teach us? Do they use us?
No. We are the masters of the myriad of things.
A part of the whole—greater than the sum of its parts—each a part of a greater universe, becoming one in itself, and nothing, while simultaneously becoming everything.

If you think of the daily items and implements you encounter and use, we can immediately know and understand that these things were created by men. Planned, designed, manufactured, distributed, marketed, sold, and used by men.

The best of us learn to use these items and implements to achieve an end, our livelihood, our career. But if men make these things, and men use these things, how can they be part of our Ultimate Embodiment with the universe?

In the Ed Tech realm we can consider devices as components of the *myriad of things*. We cannot let the myriad of things direct us, lead us, or show us. We are obliged to define the myriad of things, how they are used, as well as how they are sustained. And it is ultimately what determines achievement and success: assessment.

When the myriad of things is defined correctly, they can be used correctly. When they are used correctly, the outcomes will be achievement and success. Then the myriad of things truly becomes a critical component of the universe—of the Ultimate Embodiment.

ON DEVICES

The thing in my hands, does it give knowledge?
Does it tell things? True and false?
Do I learn it?
Does it matter if I see it, feel it, hear it?
Is it of the myriad of things?
Is it me? Is it part of the Ultimate Embodiment?
Or is it part of me? Am I part of the Ultimate Embodiment?

We know that the device, whether tablet, laptop, or smartphone, is simply an access device, a tool with a browser that allows us to access curriculum and assessment.

It could be a personal device, a take-home device, a classroom device, or a go-to device (computer lab).

We know that the user must have an understanding of the device and its use in order to derive benefit from it. Just as I must know how to sharpen a pencil, I must know how to boot the operating system and access the wireless network.

We cannot let understanding and use become the focus of devices, but we ignore these skills at the peril of those without this knowledge.

The most perilous of decisions is: "Is there one device that all can use?"

Or stated more clearly, is there one device that will fulfill all needs for all students all the time?

Obviously the answer is no. But that does not mean that we should not have devices—quite the contrary.

But this begs the larger questions about devices: what type, for whom, how to deploy, how to manage?

Can the Tao help us answer these questions?

ON SUSTAINMENT

The image I may see of a tree in the window is not a tree in the window.
The tree drinks water from the ground. It absorbs light and grows.
  The leaves fall to the ground in a never-ending cycle.
The walls of the building, the cables of the net, the devices we ride through the ether, the myriad of things, all are dynamic—expanding, changing, exhausting, dying.
How do they go on? How are they renewed? How do we know? How will they know?

No IT environment is static—change is the rule. From driver updates to software revisions to hardware upgrades to end-of-life and end-of-support—an organization's IT support environment should not be focused on systems and devices but on the life cycle of these things. These include:

- implementation and deployment
- maintenance and troubleshooting
- software upgrades and monitoring
- end-of-life and technology refresh
- call tracking, reporting, and trend analysis

The Information Technology Infrastructure Library (ITIL) defines a set of practices that focuses on aligning technology support services with business needs.

All infrastructure and technology components must be addressed in the ITIL problem management and change management policies and procedures.

Call tracking and problem management tools must be used to their fullest extent, first to address tracking problems and their resolutions, but also by analyzing the nature of problems (problem distribution) and analyzing the effectiveness of the support team over time.

These tools become the key to improvement and proactive systems management. This is the *only* way to objectively demonstrate the effectiveness of the IT organization.

Similarly, the Education Technology department is equally dynamic, but from the other side of the spectrum. The Ed Tech yang to the IT yin.

Where IT focuses on network capacity (minimize traffic), Ed Tech seeks to maximize use (increase traffic).

Where Ed Tech focuses on specific content, IT focuses on the capacity to carry any and all content.

Where IT is structured and complex, Ed Tech seeks to bring all students to their best opportunity for achievement—despite all underlying technical or societal complexity.

ON ONE TO ONE

Is the pencil the root of ideas? Is the paper the mode of communication?
Lo, does the pencil applied to paper communicate ideas?
To whom does the pencil belong? Who owns the paper?
To the novice go the myriad of things.
But does the myriad of things denote the communication of ideas?
Does mere possession of this thing obligate participation and innovation?
Is the Ultimate Embodiment more than the use of pencil on paper?

If we give the student a computer and he goes home and can't access the lesson plan because he doesn't have home WiFi, what is the school's responsibility?

Is it really the responsibility of the school to provide not only the device but the WiFi access as well?

Does the pedagogy require the use of devices and cloud-based lesson plans in order to be successful? Is this a sustainable model?

We've been studying one-to-one models going on twenty years now (1995 to 2015).

Many speak of success stories, laptop rollouts, take home iPads, ad nauseum.

But when we really get down to brass tacks (what of this idiom?), can any school or district demonstrate higher test scores and student achievement based on a one-to-one computing program? We've yet to see one.

We can see, however, examples of rising test scores when the focus is on skills, such as writing. When a school focuses like a laser on writing, supports the endeavor with professional development and training omit time, and sponsors a mentoring program, along with the addition of one-to-one devices, we have seen these examples succeed.

Is this the lynchpin for one-to-one success?

ON PARADIGM SHIFT

What of paradigm shift? What is paradigm shift?
These powerful words connote reality and movement from and to.
Does this mean the current paradigm is flawed? What is the current paradigm?
If it must shift, then to what form or function?
It is easy to call for this dynamic, but one must understand the truth and flaws of the current and address them for the future.
Presumptive? Can we define a future state that we've not experienced?
Is the new paradigm part of the Ultimate Embodiment? Or just another use of the myriad of things?

We believe that paradigm shift is necessary to achieve the ultimate goal of technology application to education. The most fundamental is the notion that technology improves education.

Technology *can* improve education, but only if the district, school, leadership, and teachers all understand the premise and concepts of the application of technology to the curriculum and can effectively practice these methods in the classroom.

Then we must still ask the same question: Have we improved student achievement?

But paradigm shift goes beyond the classroom. In fact, the paradigm shift must encompass the whole of community.

In a community where the administrators and teachers acknowledge the need to move the students to understand a new paradigm, what of their parents and community members?

Here we encounter the acknowledgment that *one* of the keys to transformation is external to the school itself. Parental communications and involvement of business and city government as well as state and federal education challenges must be addressed as well. But how?

By the organization's focus on the Ultimate Embodiment, and communication of this goal and reality throughout the school, its members, and its community.

Chapter 5

Organizational Concepts

ON ORGANIZATION

*What is this that we call Organization? Titles and lines?
  Reporting structure?
What makes it real? Who makes it real?
Does the organization act as one? Can it? Will it?
Is the organization part of the Ultimate Embodiment? Or is it just part of
  the myriad of things?*

School and school district organizations can be orderly and well managed or blanketed in utter chaos—we've seen examples of both. And no matter how chaotic the central administration, the teacher must continue to teach the students.

The question becomes, does administration serve the teachers in their efforts to serve the students? Does the district and site administration provide all the tools, training, schedule management, and infrastructure for teachers to do their job effectively?

Or do the teachers just "do the best with what they have?"

We must acknowledge that a single teacher can directly affect the test scores of her own students, but the only way to raise test scores for a whole school or district is by systematically improving every teacher's effectiveness in the classroom.

This is where the direct impact on student learning can be achieved or lost. If the superintendent provides a clear vision for each person within the district, and each teacher is empowered with best practices, techniques, and tools, then the superintendent can have a direct impact on each student's achievement—by inspiring, mentoring, and leading in a way that each individual within the hierarchy understands and works toward the same vision and goals.

ON LEADERSHIP

What of the headmaster? Is he the leader? Who do leaders lead?
Of the novices, apprentices, and enablers? Who do they follow? What do they follow?
The leader must know the Ultimate Embodiment.
The leader must communicate this plan to all.
The leader takes his role as novice, apprentice, and master. The leader is also a follower.
In the Ultimate Embodiment, we are all leaders as we are all followers.

Only two critical things are required for successful leadership: a plan and communication.

Without the plan, the leader has no context for leadership. Which way are we going? Where are we going? How will we get there?

It's not necessary that the leader have all the answers to these questions, but that he has a method to address them. It could be that many questions are to be answered, but the leader can use these questions as a context for vision and direction: strategy.

Of course, the more clear and objective the mission, goals, and objectives, the easier it is for the leader to communicate these.

But what of this communication? In our books, *N3XT Practices* and *Vision*, we reinforce the importance of communication. Of having a concise plan that all understand. That all understand not only the plan but also their scope of responsibility to achieve the plan goals.

That all help in the communication not only of the plan goals but also of the good that comes from it.

This communication must be:

- from the top
- from each department head
- consistent and frequent
- delivered with authority and respect (for the plan, its objectives, and all the players involved)

The last bullet, regarding authority and respect, becomes each party's responsibility to reflect. Nothing is more corrupting to a vision or strategy than having the players overtly or covertly question the plan and its goals.

Think of the time the IT director said, "Here's the plan *they* came up with. Even though *they* don't really know what they're doing."

This type of disclaimer or detachment will be expressed, whether intentionally or not, both up and down the organization. And it will sabotage critical communication.

ON LEADERS

What kind of leaders lead? What kind of leader do others follow?
There are four types of leaders.
The leader who leads by force.
The leader who leads by guilt and coercion.
The leader who leads by example and compassion.
The leader who leads without leading.

The *Tao Te Ching* defines the same leader aspects. The tyrant, the dominator, the teacher, and the ultimate leader—he that inspires others by his own challenges and achievement, the leader that leads without leading.

In the Ed Tech realm, the first leader—he who leads by force—is the most destructive of leaders. His staff are subject to daily scrutiny, evaluated by performance to standards and activities within constraints. Where each individual is pitted against his peers in a battle for favor and privilege. This leader destroys those around him in attempts to garner respect and authority. This leader makes demands of his subjects and punishes the failures.

The second leader takes a more subtle, manipulative approach by using the influential powers of personality and esteem to scare or coerce his subjects into his way. This power over the organization breeds distrust and internal competition. One may want to highlight their own endeavors and achievements above the greater goal of the organization, and to the detriment of those who might also gain favor. Again, this is a flaw in leadership, not of the subjects.

The third leader understands the vision and provides a pragmatic approach to achievement. By appealing to common sense, shared sacrifice, and empathy, this leader gains the respect of his subjects by treating them with respect.

By his own actions, he leads by example. Allowing others to follow his lead in applying the vision to each individual's approach. By his show of empathy and understanding, others feel at one with their leader—sharing in the sacrifice, commitment, and achievement.

This is a truly Confucianist approach.

The fourth type of leader, the "transcended leader," does so without express leadership formality, but through inspiration and love. This leader need only to exist, and by his mere existence and the communicated understanding of the Ultimate Embodiment, he inspires all others to transcend their roles in a concerted effort to become one body, a whole of community, a society of citizens.

In the Tao of Ed Tech, this transcended leader still must take the form of the school or district figurehead. And this figurehead must use express leadership formality to be successful, but he can also be the transcended leader, inspiring his community through his actions and expression and his clear understanding of the Ultimate Embodiment and expressing this by his actions and words.

ON PROFESSIONAL DEVELOPMENT

Who teaches the apprentice to teach? What is his method, his context?
How do the myriad of things allow the apprentice to teach—help the apprentice to teach? The master to lead?
How do these participants become part of the Ultimate Embodiment?

Just as education itself is a plan for indoctrinating youth to become productive members of society, so is professional development a plan to make teachers more effective at teaching using the curriculum and pedagogy of the school.

Does the school have a curriculum and pedagogy model for teachers? If the answer to this fundamental question is no, then the education services side of the house needs to get to work.

Professional development is the critical success factor for any Education Technology department. Many schools will highlight individual teacher and classroom successes. Just go to any district recognition banquet or awards event. These examples should be highlighted—the teacher's accomplishments recognized. But what beyond that? If the school or district truly advocates for the methods of this particular success, they should model the curriculum and practicum, and it should become standard curriculum and practice for the school/district—if not, then what of the recognition? Lip service?

Organizational Concepts

ON EXTERNAL FORCES

How do we deal with external forces?
Aspects given to us, for our guidance, for our benefit?
Do these external forces aid and support? They can.
Do these external forces obstruct and obscure? They can.
It is incumbent of the masters, apprentices, and enablers to encompass these external forces.
To take what they offer. To evade what they confuse. To direct what they suppose.
Do we hide from the rain? Or do we collect it and use it for our refreshment?
Do we resist these forces at our peril? Do we risk the future of the novices in our selfish arrogance?
Can we take the beneficial and ignore the impassable?
All for the Ultimate Embodiment. The external forces are of the Ultimate Embodiment, but they are not the Ultimate Embodiment.

Common Core State Standards are the perfect example of external forces.

They are defined by others (who must be more enlightened), and we are obliged to use and master them. Our novices will be measured by their achievement of these standards.

You cannot argue that the standards aren't good, only that these specific standards are not consistent with your definition of good.

Should we resist these standards? Are there good practices and aspects to these standards? What is the point of arguing and debating these?

We should know by experience that it makes no sense to resist these factors. Like getting mad at the wind.

I have found many a proponent. Schools and districts should examine and embrace the benefits of these standards.

Chapter 6

Instructional Concepts

ON COLLABORATION

What of group work? Collaboration, coordination, cultivation, collectivism.
  Do many minds work together? Can many minds work together?
Can many minds working together achieve more than the same number
  working separately?
Can the myriad of things enable? Leverage? Enhance? Transform?
Can group work help the novice achieve the Ultimate Embodiment?
  Is group work the Ultimate Embodiment?

We all know that when students collaborate, they leverage each other's knowledge, talent, and skills. With the right guidance, we've seen student work groups develop, innovate, invent, and achieve amazing things.

Can technology tools be used to support, enhance, and transform the outcomes? Yes. Do they in your environment?

Can we define and develop these curriculum and pedagogical models and effectively train all teachers in these methods?

ON PRESENTATION

We know the paradox of language. The words we use are inadequate.
They only allow what the listener has been told of the words, what the messenger understands of these words.
A picture is worth a thousand words—they say. But what of the picture? Does it communicate ideas? Facts? Truths? Answers?
There are many tools the myriad of things can offer to aid in the communication of ideas.
But the most compelling is the messenger himself. The pictures and tools must be understood and mastered in order for the messenger to successfully communicate ideas.
The tool cannot communicate these ideas by itself. This is a mistake repeated throughout time.
The message is important, The mode of communication key. The messenger critical. So we find the messenger plays a key role in the Ultimate Embodiment. But who is the messenger? Or rather, who isn't the messenger?

In today's technology-intensive classroom environment, there are truly a myriad of hardware and software tools available to enhance lesson plans, content, and, of course, student learning.

The most widely misused are the projector and screen, interactive whiteboards, and document cameras. Of course, the most maligned and misused software is Microsoft PowerPoint. That is not to say that any of these tools cannot be invaluable, only that the promise of professional development and modeling has—for the most part—failed in the classroom.

We all have seen success stories—individual successes at each school or district. However, the scenario breaks down when the district spends large amount of money on deploying these technologies to every classroom without functional and creative professional development for each teacher in a timely manner.

There is nothing worse than watching a teacher read from a bland slide deck the same sentences and syllabi that the teacher used to have in MS Word as handouts.

Graphics, streaming video, interactive tools, and video conferencing are all advanced media types that can enhance any presentation. There are also some common denominators: large and multiple viewable screens, audio amplification of all sources, and remote sharing of the video projection.

But we must acknowledge one thing—and no teacher will disagree—the teacher is *the* critical component in the equation. *And* a good teacher could teach any class without any presentation tools. They did all through time.

ON DIGITAL CITIZENSHIP

We know the Golden Rule. Humanity's ultimate truths hold in the technical world, and in the Ultimate Embodiment.

The question becomes, "How do we know these truths?" Are they taught to us? Are they defined in a great text?

It is the job of the masters to define the rules, and communicate them throughout their organization. For all, the novices, apprentices, and enablers live by the rules.

For to assume these rules are known and understood is to do so at the peril of all associated.

By defining the rules, and communicating the rules, the Ultimate Embodiment can transcend these rules and their symptoms and mitigate the behavior.

The Tao recognizes that the truths of life also apply to the truths of living in the digital world. It also acknowledges that the rules of digital citizenship, although they may be straightforward and "common sense," they must be formalized and communicated. Teachers and administrators cannot assume that students know, understand, and follow the rules.

It is clearly the responsibility of school administration to define the rules of digital citizenship for all within the school district. To provide the tools to communicate them, to the students, through the teachers.

One would hope that once all participants are indoctrinated into the acceptable behavior in the digital world, then a presumption of understanding would take place. And society can encompass the Ultimate Embodiment.

But we cannot deny the need to embrace, emphasize, and communicate the explicit rules to all parties (not just the students), frequently and throughout the organization.

ON ETHICAL BEHAVIOR

How do we know of ethics? Is it a rule or law? Is it nature's law?
How do we understand ethics? How do we teach others to
  understand ethics? Are we obliged to define ethics?
Why must we teach ethics? Is it nature's law?
How do these ethics apply to the myriad of things?
Are ethics part of the Ultimate Embodiment? Of course!

We cannot delve into an academic study of Ethics. Although this is a kind of a philosophy book, we will deal with the noncapitalized form (ethics). But we can ask the most fundamental questions regarding moral and natural law, and the concept of good and bad. What could be a better yin yang study?

Even though we can immediately understand how ethics omit and ethical behavior apply in the technology realm, we must also ask the following questions:

- Should we define the ethical use of technology systems?
- How do we communicate these definitions or guidelines?
- How do we enforce these ethics?
- Do we reward or punish good or bad ethics? If so, how?

ON SOCIAL NETWORKS

Who are you? What are you? What do others think of you?
  Is perception reality?
Are you good or bad? Happy or sad? Fat or thin? Thus the yin yang of the
  social network.
We must acknowledge the bad, and harvest the good. We must control the
  perception that becomes our reality. For what the page tells of you is
  what you allow.

A wise man once said, "it is better to keep your mouth closed, and have others think you are a fool, than to open it and remove all doubt."

Thus is the rule for the social networks. What you allow to define you, others will misread and misunderstand. What you might find as good, others see as bad. Your attributes, flaws. Your skills, liabilities. Your best wishes, narcissistic indulgences.

Much good has been attained via the social network, and much bad has manifested to balance the scale. But it is possible to find the good, and leave the bad to those who would not exercise better judgment. It is a lesson for all, but most importantly, for the apprentice to teach the novice. For the novice is the most likely to fall into the pit of acrimony offered by the social network.

ON LEARNING MANAGEMENT SYSTEMS

What is the ultimate learning tool? The environment that supports all learning? Does it exist?

This tool must provide for the novice, his daily lesson, the schedule of lessons, the collaboration with others, the communication with masters and apprentices, the archive of past history, the story of my achievement, the best of my best.

Learning management systems are becoming more and more ubiquitous in the education realm. These are tools that can foster the work between teacher, students, and work groups. It supports collaboration, communication, submission, review, assessment, and interactive messaging. It has a calendar of events and topical information. It provides access to learning tools and content.

The most important factor is teacher utilization. If these tools are put in place, the students can only use as much as the teacher allows the LMS to facilitate. Professional development, once again, becomes the key to efficacy. Use by all can only be achieved if there is access to all—if everyone has the device and connectivity to access the environment.

ON PEDAGOGY

Can we teach learning? Can we teach teaching?
Is there one way to learn? Can there be one way to teach?
Can different novices learn differently? Can different apprentices teach differently?
If the novice achieves, then does it matter?
Can we model the achievement? Can we model the teaching?
What of the myriad of things? Are they part of learning and teaching?
Pedagogy is not the Ultimate Embodiment, but if effective, it becomes part of the Ultimate Embodiment.

We can only discuss pedagogy in the context of Education Technology within the scope of this book. But the same inquiry applies both within and in the more general educational context. We can all agree that students learn differently, and teachers teach differently. And as long as the outcomes are positive, how can we decide on methodology, or rather, pedagogy?

In the technology realm, how do hardware devices and software interfaces restrict or achieve greater understanding or enhanced learning?

DATA ANALYSIS AND DECISION SUPPORT SYSTEMS

What of data? What data is useful? For the apprentice? What data can be provided? What does it explain? How does the apprentice know? How does it impact the novice?
Is it part of the myriad of things or the Ultimate Embodiment?

Schools these days must use assessment data and decision support systems to be able to analyze, compare, make decisions, and impact efficacy and productivity, and ultimately student achievement.

Data warehouses and decision support systems are developed to compile and compare information that was not easily accessible in the past. Although the data existed in various databases and systems, they were never integrated to provide comprehensive assessment data, combined with student information, statewide and districtwide data and demographics. With these real-time, data-driven capabilities, teachers must be able to review assessment results and affect or modify their curriculum and/or pedagogy to best impact their student's individual achievement.

And although many districts have implemented these systems, the more impactful questions are, have the teachers been trained on how to:

- access the data
- understand each data type and where it comes from
- understand the state and district metrics
- understand how to adjust or affect their future delivery based on this data
- understand what impacts are expected from leadership

ON THE EDUCATION TECHNOLOGY DEPARTMENT

Who are the enablers we call Education Technology? What is their role? What is their scope? Why is technology part of their role?
Are they of the myriad of things? I think not. Are they of the Ultimate Embodiment?
If they are of the Ultimate Embodiment, then they have no role, no scope—they simply are.

The enablers we know of as Education Technology are of the department focused on assisting teachers by helping them use technology to enhance curriculum. They are immersed in developing a model for technology application to district curriculum. They provide the professional development for teachers to understand the use of classroom technology tools, instructional applications and learning systems, data analysis and decision-support tools, and of course, a district-based model that is focused on curriculum goals and student outcomes.

They work closely with the IT department to form a seamless model from desktop and technology support, through student information, and instructional applications support.

Although they teach the effective use of the many available tools and techniques available, they cannot make the teachers develop, share, and use technology-based content.

Oftentimes we see Ed Tech departments offering training without the ability to offer stipends or subtime. Offerings are attended lightly, and few standards are communicated and thus used. It is almost as if the Ed Tech department is creating work for itself. In this instance, the Ed Tech department is part of the myriad of things—just another requirement the teacher doesn't have time to deal with, and since participation is not enforced, there is no accountability.

We see professional development, and the PD program, as the key to overall success. Not of the myriad of things but of the Ultimate Embodiment. Thus, the PD program is a critical puzzle piece of Education Technology's role in education, and education's role in community, and therefore society.

Especially as advanced assessment tools, data reporting, and decision support systems are implemented, it becomes a critical success factor that all teachers and administrators can use and benefit from.

ON CONTENT DEVELOPMENT

What does it mean to standardize content development? Are standards really constraints? Are templates really restrictions?

In the yin yang of curriculum development there must be a natural balance between what is best communicated by the apprentice, and what is similar for all novices to benefit equally.

The content must align with external forces and focus on the novice's endeavor.

What one develops, others should be able to use and leverage. Therefore, the entity must compile, manage, and make it available to all.

Wherein this vast store of content is easy to navigate, easy to incorporate, easy to leverage, not just by apprentices, not just one of the myriad of things, but for the Ultimate Embodiment.

The development of curricular content is one of the great yin yang conundrums of technology since computers were introduced. When elaborate content development systems have been introduced (at great cost to many districts), the teachers didn't have training or time to spend migrating their current Word documents to this proprietary platform—many districts purchased Content Management Systems (CMS)—a software system that provided standardized tools and templates for content development, and a standardized delivery platform. Unfortunately, most districts weren't able to train their teachers in the development method and were not able to develop a model to incentivize teachers to develop and share content.

On the other side of the coin, when powerful tools with less structure are introduced, teachers go wild in developing content, but consistency within this vast library of content is nonexistent. Just take a browse around Smart's Exchange library of curriculum built using Smart Notebook software. You can literally find anything you may want to teach, but alignment with CCSS and any type of district standards are always in question.

So the district/school must deal with providing a platform for allowing teachers to migrate existing content and develop new content, without restricting their freedom to incorporate rich media types. At the same time, professional development and coaching must ensure that new content aligns with Common Core and fundamentally focuses on improving student outcomes and achievement.

Finally, and this is where the school or district really must step up to the plate in terms of commitment and resources ($), the district must provide a common platform for all users to access, stream, and leverage any and all content that has been developed and is available, through a secure and common interface. That means resources dedicated to the operation, storage, management, and sustainment of an electronic storehouse of digital content.

Think of your district's own private YouTube of curriculum videos and content. This could be in a public or private cloud.

Chapter 7

Technical Concepts

ON THE INFORMATION TECHNOLOGY DEPARTMENT

Who are the enablers we know as IT? What is their role, their scope?
Their roads and bridges are not bricks and mortar, but glass and copper.
  Their tools are not hammers and ploughs, but meters and monitors.
  They don't hammer and grade, they configure and optimize.
The users fly their devices near and far. To the same and different worlds.
  By themselves and with others. Accessing the domain of the myriad of
  things, becoming part of the Ultimate Embodiment.
And though their tools and roads are part of the myriad of things, they
  truly enable the Ultimate Embodiment. And unlike other enablers,
  accountability is direct and immediate.
Lo, the IT enabler that cannot respond to the urgent need. Though they are
  part of a whole, their scope is the road upon which all travel.

Thus the Tao of Ed Tech advocates for the criticality of the IT department. In their role as the operational support entity of all things technology related—which are all things—we find that every aspect of school district operations becomes reliant on access to the applications, databases, email, and the Internet. Therefore, *any* interruption to access to the network or network performance is deemed an IT issue, and the IT department must be ready and able to jump into action and fix any and all problems and related issues. And when nontechnical issues are blamed on technical platforms, the IT department must be able to assign and escalate as the trouble will undoubtedly be theirs to fix.

ITIL is the body of processes and industry best practices required to best support operational IT environments. IT can be divided into operations and strategy. The operations component is the support organization. This is typically a reactive troubleshooting team that is assigned by expertise as problems arise. They may use tools to resolve those problems. This is the Tier-1 problem management side of IT.

The strategy component is the planning or proactive site of the organization. It plans for future implementations and resources. It mitigates problems before they occur. This is the change management side of IT.

ON TECHNOLOGY STANDARDS

What is this standard? To whom do the standards belong? By whom are the standards defined? How often do the standards change?

Who benefits from the standards? Who enforces the standards? What is the penalty if the standards are violated?

Are the standards part of the myriad of things?

Technology standards are a complicated issue. If the questions above cannot be easily answered, then a complete assessment and plan needs to be developed to understand the impact (or lack) the implementation of standards may have.

If examined one by one, we will see quickly and clearly that the issue of developing standards, publicizing them, and enforcing them may be a slippery slope that only serves to prove that the standards are not only meaningless but also unenforceable. Especially if the standards impact equipment not being purchased by the group setting the standards. "If it's not your money, then it's none of your business." Although we know this is not true, are you willing to test this premise? At what risk? At whose peril?

Once again, the implementation of "standards" must be acknowledged and endorsed by leadership. The discussion of enforcement and penalty must be had. Normally answered, "There is none."

The first thing that leadership might realize in this discussion is that these standards are much ado about nothing, and not worth the web page they are written on. Who is going to risk their political capital over a technology standard? Maybe *guideline* is really a better word and idea.

ON CLOUD COMPUTING

What is the cloud? Where is this cloud? Who owns the cloud?
Is the cloud ever-present? Is it ultimately reliable? Can everyone access the cloud?
Is the cloud of the myriad of things? Nothing more, nothing less.

You might be asking the following questions:

- Do we need to move to the cloud?
- How do I know if we need to move to the cloud?
- What would we move to the cloud?
- How do we move to the cloud?

First of all, don't get intimidated. The main thing to remember regarding the cloud is that the cloud is storage and computing resources available on the Internet.

Which also means that once your organization moves to the cloud, those services will become totally dependent on access to these cloud services via the Internet.

The other main business consideration of moving to the cloud is Opex versus Capex (operational expenditure versus capital expenditure). Moving from internal infrastructure and hosts to cloud-based services will eliminate capital expenditures on hardware and licensing and convert them to operational expenses, managed on a monthly or annual basis. These factors will impact cash flow and your organization's balance sheet.

This also fundamentally impacts your organization's ownership of its datasince data in the cloud is no longer on your premises. Business continuity and disaster recovery plans must change to accommodate the change in architecture.

Similarly, your organization's IT support operations needs will change since there will be no more local servers, server admins, UPS, backups, viruses, and more. That's not to say these services/resources aren't required, they just may be engaged via service-level agreements and no longer be payroll employees.

The most convenient time to consider cloud services is when procuring or implementing a new platform. For instance—moving to a new Student Information System (SIS) or a new Learning Management System (LMS) might be a good time to consider the cloud. This also allows your organization to test cloud-based services before moving the entire organization to the new platform.

The next opportunity to start your inquiry into the cloud is when your IT staff starts talking about purchasing new hardware: servers, storage, and others. This event will provide the opportunity to compare hard numbers and monthly service fees.

ON INTERNET CONNECTIVITY

What of the Internet? How are we connected to the Internet? It is a simple question, but a difficult answer.
What is needed from the Internet? Why? What of bandwidth? Filtering? Security?
What is the connection between the cloud and the Internet? What does one have to do with the other?
This connection, the Internet Connection, may be the most oversubscribed, technology component within the district. Live or die by it. It is the last bottleneck of performance.

Never has the need for more bandwidth become so urgent as today, driven by educational one-to-one and bring your own device (BYOD) programs.

We're not talking about incremental or even geometric growth—we're talking about exponential growth—think hockey-stick chart.

That's what happens when your school implements wireless and goes from one computer for every teacher to a laptop for every student (and realistically, we know that many students may have as many as three wireless devices).

As Educational Technologists, we seek to design and implement the most cost-effective, yet robust, architectures possible to support future growth.

In the past, we've seen the network bottleneck move from the network edge to the network core to the WAN (Wide Area Network), then to the WAP (Wireless Application Protocol) and around again.

But as we push 10Gbps at the network core and theoretical multilink throughput beyond 1Gbps with 802.11ac, the final network bottleneck at your school district will likely end up in one location—you guessed it—the Internet link.

The modeling is actually simple arithmetic. Let's say you're a small district with ten schools, four hundred teachers, and five thousand students (if we completely ignore the counts of staff and administrative computers, which used to outnumber the classroom computers). This would mean your network would grow from 400 computers to 5,400 computers through a one-to-one initiative. That's 1,350 percent growth!

So if we assume you've implemented 1Gbps to the WAP, 10Gbps at the LAN core, and 1Gbps on the WAN, anything less than 1Gbps to the Internet (through your ISP) will undoubtedly become the final bottleneck.

This problem will be exacerbated by the number of students using cloud-based applications. Traffic patterns will no longer spike at 8 a.m. and 2 p.m., they'll be hitting peaks throughout the day.

So what can we do after we've maxed out both our capital and operational budgets for networking equipment and ISP services?

1. Implement data center and private cloud storage. Use it for collaboration and student file storage. Storage will continue to become cheaper and faster.
2. Implement as many private cloud applications as possible. If instructional and collaboration applications can be hosted within the district private cloud, reliance on the Internet can be significantly reduced.

I know this is easier said than done (ESTD), with GAFE (Google Apps for Education) and most LMS (Learning Management Systems) being cloud based. But you as Ed Tech director must consider these options. Many SIS and LMS systems today offer private cloud licensing.

3. Filter, filter, filter. The more limitations you put on your filtered guest/student wireless, the more you can cut down on Internet traffic.
4. Train teachers and students to store multimedia and video files in the private cloud.
5. Increase operational budgets for ISP bandwidth every year. Another ESTD.

I usually don't like to be pessimistic, but the only sure thing is this: this bottleneck will not be eliminated by school districts in the near future.

ON BUSINESS CONTINUITY

It is the scope of the enablers to prepare the "systems" for constant operation. For all are reliant on the systems and the systems are reliant on all the infrastructure and technologies.

The IT enabler therefore must plan for the elimination of all points of failure. And in doing so, the enabler will ensure the viability of the system.

Where the system is a chain only as strong as its weakest link, he follows a method of identifying possible failures and eliminating them.

Without this practice, the Ultimate Embodiment and the myriad of things may be rendered useless by a single failure.

He tests these preparations for validity and reliability.

Lo, the failure of technology from lack of preparation becomes the failure of the myriad of things and the Ultimate Embodiment.

ON DISASTER RECOVERY

We must have a plan for the worst case. But do we know the worst case? Individual failures among the myriad of things is not the worst case. The worst case is when everything is no longer as it was—where all assumptions are wrong—where all bets are off.
How do we plan for the worst case? How can we continue?

Disaster Recovery (DR) and Business Continuity (BC) could be one of the most overlooked aspects of Information Technology planning and implementation.

BC is in the context of eliminating single-points-of-failure (SPOF). In the high-availability design environment, each component in the computing, network, and storage areas is designed and implemented with layers of redundancy. The more critical your IT systems (I don't know of any school districts that haven't become totally dependent on their IT stuff), the more business continuity needs need to be addressed.

DR must be considered in the context of "what will we do if the district office burns down?" Any and all levels of BC can be rendered meaningless in the case of some disaster that takes out the whole building. For instance, if the building housing your data center were destroyed, what would be required to bring "critical" systems back online? SIS, email, and transportation/GIS systems would need to be back online first. Is there a complete backup of data, applications software, operating systems images that could be brought into production on some standard hardware? Is the original media available to create scratch OS builds? Are the OS build procedures documented? Or is your hardware platform so customized that it couldn't be replicated no matter what? That really means that in a disaster, you couldn't come back up in weeks or even months.

To be clear, DR is a subset of BC. BC seeks to identify all likely points of failure (POF) and implement equipment, processes, and procedures to address each one.

Several BC components are implemented automatically as you plan your next server upgrade. For instance, RAID technology within your SAN (storage area network) insures that individual hard drive failures don't affect BC by monitoring drive status, providing alerts in the event of failure, and allowing your IT guy to replace the drives using hot-swap technology.

Take a systematic top-down or bottom-up approach and review each possible POF. Then address each according to its level of criticality. Obviously, this means an assessment of criticality comes first. Start with a BC and DR plan. Then create the implementation plan. Procure each component and implement with BC and DR in mind—you don't want your BC project to trigger your DR plan.

Verify BC and DR Practices

Finally, verification of BC and DR practices are rarely performed. We don't need to discuss why it isn't done—convenience, opportunity, downtime—but the risk of not planning and documenting a full recovery operation only ensures that when, or if, this disaster happens, the organization really doesn't know if the process and procedures will actually work. You can't know unless you test it—all of it.

Chapter 8

Operational Concepts

ON HELP DESK (TIER 1)

How do we fix a problem? Who fixes problems? Does each know who? What is the role of Tier 1? Is it clearly defined?

The help desk is the first point of contact of problem management. Every IT operation needs a functional "help desk." It need not be a physical desk, but a first point of contact from the troubled user to the IT organization. It is often referred to as Tier 1—the first tier of support—the first point of contact.

Several things should happen when the user calls (or emails, or enters his problem on the web):

1. The end user must receive acknowledgment that the call was received.
2. The time should be stamped.
3. A ticket number should be assigned.
4. The problem description should be taken.
5. An initial classification of the trouble should be determined.
6. The urgency or criticality of the trouble should be determined—typically by the number of users affected.

The help desk then would take the first steps to troubleshoot and/or resolve the problem from the desk using remote control and desktop administration tools.

The help desk process must be supported by a calltracking system, which should include a knowledge-based engine that allows all historical trouble calls to be categorized and their resolutions stored for later reference.

ON PROBLEM MANAGEMENT

How do we fix problems? We employ enablers, specialists, experts. How do they know of problems? It is the role of the system to log, assign, track, compile, resolve problems. When all things are working, when all things are good.

But the system is more than sustainment. It also holds the metrics for measurement, analysis, comparison, and improvement.

Let constant improvement be the benefit of this system, part of the myriad of things.

This call tracking system should be the core work management tool for all operations—not just IT operations, but in many cases, IT call tracking is separate from work order call tracking. The point is, IT operations—the reactive side of the house—must have a robust call tracking system that allows users to call in, email, or log trouble calls directly via the web. Once entered, the Tier-1 resource must acknowledge, classify type and priority, provide first-line assessment and troubleshooting, and if not immediately resolved, assign it to the appropriate resource.

Once assigned, the tracking system will have mandatory interactions with the assigned resources and age the ticket. This should be followed through to the resolution, where the problem is solved, the resolution entered into the knowledge base, the user informed, and the ticket closed.

But this is just the core operations of the system. The benefits derived must be exploited to truly leverage these systems, including knowledge base, monthly reporting of call statistics, problem distribution, trend analysis, and resource performance and productivity.

Truly, this system should become the lifeblood of any enterprise-class IT Operations environment.

ON CHANGE MANAGEMENT

Change is constant. But change should not mean trouble. Change should not cause problems. If we know of coming change, we can act to mitigate trouble. If we understand the needed change, even the most difficult changes can be managed.
Lo, communication can mitigate problems caused by change. Or we can be victims of change.

As a key component of IT strategy, change management is the proactive, planning, and strategic process in IT. If we are changing, implementing, and upgrading, then we know what the impacts will be. We know who will be impacted. We know how.

This knowledge, and this information, by itself, can be the difference between a successful implementation or a failed implementation.

If your deployment team has to go out and do a switch upgrade and accidentally takes the administration building down, that is a failed implementation. But if the team knows they will take the building switches down and schedules this on off hours, then the exact same project may be deemed a total success, merely by managing the change, the impacts, and the impacted.

ON KNOWLEDGE BASE

What if we could compile all the troubles of the past, and record the resolutions? We could look back at the data, and use it to improve our collective support role. The data will enhance the ability of the enablers, thereby enhancing the experience of all.

What if we don't? Have we lost the opportunity to gain from our past? To learn as we have already learned? To improve upon our past performance?

It is part of the myriad of things, a tool for the enablers, a key for the Ultimate Embodiment.

Any proper help desk and/or call tracking/work order system must have a knowledge base capability. This is the ability to store and classify all the past trouble reports and make them available to whomever is working on the help desk. It should be noted that if the Tier-2 technician was able to fix it remotely, then the help desk or Tier-1 technician should be able to do it remotely next time, thereby eliminating the need to assign the problem to a Tier-2 specialist and reducing the call resolution time.

ON TREND ANALYSIS

How else may we use this compilation of trouble? This history of failure? Can we look at the collection of trouble through a period, and find more fundamental problems, trouble at the core?
View the historical data over a time period, and the data will speak directly to anyone looking. The trouble may not be trouble at all, or just a better organization of the myriad of things.

The help desk data, over time, presents the best opportunity for an IT department to analyze, assess, and strategize for enterprise improvement. What does that mean? If you analyze help desk data over time, trends will arise, which may expose fundamental or systemic issues that are causing help desk calls.

For example, the IT department noticed that printing problems would spike up for periods of time, and then settle down. Months later this would reoccur. When examined month by month, not much attention would be paid to the matter. But when analyzed on an annualized basis, it could be seen that these issues would spike each quarter, in time with scheduled application updates, meaning that when scheduled updates occurred, printing configurations needed to be reconfigured. Without the trend review, these two conditions might never be associated.

ON REPORTING

Are we too busy? Is there too much work, or too few enablers? Thus is the quandary of the IT enablers. Often too busy, but by what measure? Often away, but where?

If projects do not cause problems, then the IT enablers do not get more work from these projects. Their time must be managed by workload and expertise.

How do we compare those who work on change from those who work on problems?

How do we balance their workloads? How can they help each other?

How do they support the myriad of things? How can we best measure their collective performance as well as their individual performance? Why?

Help desk statistics reporting is the critical information base of any IT department. The key to which is, of course:

1. having a comprehensive help desk call tracking system
2. having processes and procedures to insure that all users and all support personnel know how to use the system
3. utilizing structured and periodic reporting to measure results—including the ability to compare performance between IT staff

Any time I review an IT organization, the first question I ask is: "What is the average call resolution time?" If the IT director cannot answer this question, then all the above help desk tracking and call statistics aren't being used. Worse yet, is the data being collected?

Another important matter is workload. If an IT director tells me that his staff is "overworked," I ask, "What is the average call load per technician?" If the IT director doesn't know this, then any sense of being "overworked" is unfounded.

This type of reporting is the key to unlocking the dysfunction within an IT department.

Average Calls per Month (or Day) is a key metric for the IT department as a whole, and then for each technical resource. It may be normal for Tier 1 to resolve ten calls per day or for the network engineer to resolve one call per day, but your department will never know the norm without collecting and comparing these statistics month by month.

If your IT resources are assigned by site, this metric will become very important. It can be used to best manage the time for each resource, but what you may find out is that unless they are remote distances away, IT resources are best operating at a central location and dispatched to sites accordingly. It would not be surprising that the high school may need dedicated resources, whereas multiple elementary schools might share a single resource. But without comparing call loads and resolution times, this balance cannot be achieved and maintained.

The passage also refers to the difference in workload and type between help desk, or problem resources, and projects and change management resources.

It is not uncommon for engineering resources, especially at Tiers 2 and 3 that work on both, to do problem management and change management (or problems and projects).

If a network engineer spends half his time working on a new routing project (change), he cannot be expected to have the same call load or average call resolution times as his help desk peers.

That doesn't mean that his statistics shouldn't be measured, only that the metrics will differ. In fact, don't let these resources off the hook. If someone knows they aren't being measured while others are, then you will encourage an elite class within your organization.

Chapter 8

ON CONSTANT IMPROVEMENT

The best true goal for any organization is to improve. Improve what? you say. Improve by what? Improve how?

All these are good, truth-seeking questions. This is not true of the IT enablers only, the Ed Tech enablers only, but it is true for all. Any and all should seek improvement. In all things for all purposes.

In order to improve we must establish metrics, the mode of data collection, a standard of process and procedure for all, communicated to all, leveraged and understood by all.

It is the true embodiment of all things for the individual and the community to seek to improve. It is all reliant on the fourth form of leadership. Of the true symbiosis of community. As we improve we all grow and become part of the Ultimate Embodiment.

Constant improvement is truly a noble goal. At every level, for every person, in every aspect of their life.

But without being too ethereal, it is easy to recognize that someone, or something, must take charge to implement the measures and metrics, and communicate them to all within the organization. Each individual must understand that his or her performance is being measured, and improvement sought.

What does that mean for the:

- help desk?
Reducing the average call resolution time.
- Tier-1 and Tier-2 resources?
Increase average calls per day and reduce average call resolution times.
- IT director?
Reduction of call loads via proactive management and trend analysis and training.

Producing monthly reports of:

- average call resolution times
- average call load
- average call resolution times per resource
- average call load per resource

Conclusion

ON THE ULTIMATE EMBODIMENT

Have we learned of the Ultimate Embodiment? Have we always known the Ultimate Embodiment? Just as the newborn knows only survival.

Are we of the Ultimate Embodiment? We are, inasmuch as we are participants in the universal whole. Are we victims? Prisoners? Strangers among men? Or are we discoverers, pioneers, educators, practitioners, entrepreneurs, leaders? We are what we choose, if we choose. In our role as novice.

What of the novice? What is their role in the Ultimate Embodiment?

This question holds the key—to the paradox, the conundrum, the yin yang, the myriad of things, and of course, the Ultimate Embodiment.

He is the key to the universe, and those who serve him allow him to inherit the fruits of all our labor.

About the Author

Darryl Vidal has been consulting for schools implementing technology for over twenty years. His projects include districtwide implementations of VoIP, wireless, data center virtualization, and video security. His primary instructional focus for over fifteen years has been the ever-evolving technology classroom. Mr. Vidal has developed the formal strategic planning and project management methodology known as MapIT[sm]. He is currently the vice president and principal Education Technology consultant for the Southern California–based technology firm Networld Solutions, Inc.